Naming
Stones

Mary Griffiths

ISBN: 978 0 993 0186 2 6

CONTENTS

For Emma, with love and gratitude

This book comes from a lifetime of working with literature, both as a student and a teacher, so my thanks are due to all those who have shared with me their love of poetry. Members of the sangha at the Manchester Buddhist Centre have been central to the development of my creative life as part of my spiritual practice, so I offer this book for the benefit of all sentient beings.

Chesil Beach

He had been buried,

but we three chose a different farewell.

It seemed right for him, Chesil Beach.

The sea always soothed his senses,

for a while, drowned his sorrows

for a while, 'though not enough.

Early morning sunshine on the water,

gulls crying, Martha and the Muffins,

Echo Beach playing, moving poetry.

Candles, flowers strewn on the water,

futile pebbles collected for his grave.

Tears. An almost perfect ritual.

Then, trudging up the slope,

stumbling for home,

the pebbles grabbed her shoe.

We could see it and turned,

moved back down to save it.

All three of us scrabbled to save it,

with strange, wrenching laughter;

but the unrelenting, all-engulfing,

griefless pebbles closed in.

It was gone, and no amount of frantic,

hopeless delving could bring it back.

Still, for a long time we could not stop.

Pushchair

That time my mind fell asleep

Kindness watched intently,

like a mother with her wayward toddler,

strapped in her pushchair,

so long unable to rest,

but at last sound asleep,

body twisted, head aslant,

snotty nose, jagged breath,

but still.

Asleep after all the tantrums, the fighting,

the long, hard days.

Doormat

When the prop collapsed

his clothes fell on to the muddy earth.

She trampled on them.

Trampled, stamped and crushed them

into the ground.

So my mother told me.

I can see her, small, balled-up.

A Fury – the softly-spoken, mild Bella –

My grandmother.

She trampled him under her tiny bound feet.

Survivor

I never knew you there on the pavement

as the blacklegs scuttle unobtrusively towards the pit.

You yell, shake your fists. A Fury.

Your timid, jail-fearing family hold you back.

I wondered at your energy.

Was it twelve or thirteen

children you held?

My father varied it

from tale to tale.

Five did not survive.

Perhaps you thought *thirteen* unlucky.

You were, you might say, unlucky enough.

Mild, drunken husband,

Poverty, black pats scuttling

down the cracked stone floor at night.

Such stories I was steeped in.

What absorbed me, 'though,

Was not the coal-black hardship,

But your shining.

Your silent laughter, belly shaking,

"The cemetery shovel's after me, doctor!"

Loving thirteen.

Your domestic courage, Catherine.

I smile.

Your diamond DNA tucked inside me,

Somewhere.

Heirloom (for E. and H.)

I'd like to wrap you in my magic shawl,

the one with the large blue 'M' on it.

It is ancient, a gift from your grandmother,

grown from the spells cast over it,

There, there; never mind; this will pass; God Bless.

Its strong weave can keep at bay

some Swords and Dragons,

Sleep tight; good girl; love you; kiss it better.

Sometimes its cosiness can warm a Frozen Heart,

and when the Damp Ghosts clutch at you

its heat can evaporate them,

its scent can heal when other Potions fail.

This shawl can unravel; it's showing

signs of wear and tear, so mend and tend it carefully –

it is the best I can bequeath you.

Crumpled

Did you know that you can

vacuum-pack a love?

Squash it, make it small,

with all the air squeezed out.

Shove it under the bed, out of the way.

It won't take up too much space.

It will be crumpled, can't be helped.

Sometime it may be wanted again.

Maybe then you can let it out,

let it take a gasping breath,

assume its proper size,

its proper place.

The Demon Drink

I did not mean to come and see you dead,

but find myself here, viewing your papyrus face.

Through lidded eyes, a gorgon's stare.

Body (wasted, I know), shrouded.

Beyond the door is laden

with the nurse's tip-toeing expectation

of grief and sorrow,

my ageing companions.

Had I hoped for solace?

Rest in Peace?

This face is rigid, determined

not to yield, to see, to go.

Clenched, rusted will

drained you to the dregs.

When death came,

you would have raged, I know.

After Alexander McQueen

1.

I catwalk into dark theatres,

tall in my split-skirt puritan cavalier ensemble.

My Oxfam textiles meet

silly-money-ed haute couture.

My stitches fall apart, contemplating

his awesome, glittering scissors.

2.

Faceless,

she's clothed in terrible flowers,

overflowing sleeves, creeping up

her stalk-like neck.

Strangling, straining blossoms

bulge through diaphanous shrouds,

a sinister abundance of jungled beauty

leeches my breath away.

3.

Gasping, shocked by beauty, rough hessian

over vulnerable, brittle-boned lace.

Through the intricate, embroidered flowers

I smell the blood from the finger pricked sewing them.

4.

Through the charcoal depths

on my way to masquerades

in this realm of lurid loveliness

I float in beauty, soft in my

sanguinary-feathered gown.

I hobble in my grotesque,

cloven armadillo heels.

In my glittering, gem-encrusted head

I'm smelling the musky snouts

of predators encircling me.

Hurt

You never stab me

in the heart.

No dramatic gushing

fountain of blood.

No crumpling to the floor.

No ambulances.

Just paper-cuts.

Lots of them.

After Jenny Joseph

When I am divorced I shall eat garlic,

and sleep diagonally across the double bed.

I shall have complete control of the remote,

and never watch a football match again.

I shall summon a craftsman to do the DIY,

and avoid expletive-laden wonky shelves.

I shall never shave my legs. I will grow hair wherever I like.

I shall read in bed 'til all hours, eating crisps.

Always keep the toilet seat down.

Never have shelves of lager in the fridge.

Cover the sofa with as many cushions

as I damn well like.

Throw out the collection of beer mats.

But until then, we have to share the duvet,

and wear ear plugs to get a good night's sleep,

and laugh loyally at the same old jokes,

and show gratitude for the thoughtless birthday gifts,

the endless scented candles and the scentless flowers.

Ancestry

We met and it seemed like love.

Drifting blindly into the familiar,

the interlocking attachment.

Pieces of an ancient jigsaw,

dovetailed now in our

inherited picture of misery.

I desperately want you

not to be a passing thing,

to have and to hold,

breathlessly knowing

there's no having, no holding.

The syntax is off, the rhyme broken.

In our duo the harmony is smashed

by ego-clashing tinny notes of

echoing loneliness.

Puppets

When the thumbnail digs into

the fruit of anger,

the acid splash stains anyone.

Then guilt, old man of the sea,

image of implacable sorrow, weight on shoulders.

Eyes forced to the ground.

Every step strains, drains energy,

smothers joy. You taunt with brief relief

as you slither off for a while,

but I hear your footsteps, Gollum-like behind,

know you have a part to play

as you leap back on and damn me,

pointing with my own index finger.

Colouring In

You are the orange Smartie©,

the last seat on the train,

the first day of holidays,

umbrella when it rains.

A wink of understanding,

a grin from ear to ear,

rescue in the nick of time,

salt within a tear.

This smile, this huge expanding smile,

will crack my face for love of you.

Relief

Quaffing my celebratory drink

I glance out of the pub window

at the freefalling, sky-diving rain.

I long to dash outside,

singing in the rain.

Relief is such a potent draught

I feel I want everything

to dance with me.

Fear had parched my mouth,

tight-lipped, I could not speak,

still less sing a word.

Relief, heartsease, honeyed lozenge,

soothed my watering mouth.

My voice returns, cracked, halting,

but one day will sing songs again.

Healthy

End stress today.

Lose weight.

Get younger skin.

Declutter your life.

Go Dairy-free.

Calcium for osteoporosis.

Move more.

Don't rush.

Vitamin D vital for health. Get more sun.

Malignant melanoma. Get less sun.

Ten filling low-carb dishes

(You just eat the crockery, get it?)

Eat raw.

Fifteen ways to get a happy

Life/Gut/Sex Partner/Delete as appropriate.

Confused, overloaded?

Recycle.

Keep it simple.

Don't buy it.

Thin

Roundness, so touchable,

cushion-like,

sheltering of fragile bone,

is anathema to you.

Angular is sophisticated,

tightly controlled.

Deadly fashionable.

Dead fashionable.

Street Life

'He should pull himself together.'

'She'll just spend it on booze.'

'Fancy keeping a dog when you're homeless.'

'Soap doesn't cost anything.'

'Beggars cluttering our streets.'

'With all the tax we pay.'

'They should do something about it.'

'We should do something about it.'

'The problem, not Them, you understand.'

'Keep it neutral. Agenda-less.'

'Tick the box for "suffering" and close the file.'

Who said soundbite simplicity

can't mask pain's complicity?

On Retreat

It always happens.

There's always one

you don't like the look of,

who presses your buttons,

who doesn't like you.

Time passes.

The Buddha's silence changes things,

to a new, brief story.

This time, pouring rain,

outdoor walkway to the shrine,

she waits for you, umbrella up.

You rush to join her,

wrap your arms around one another,

and run, laughing, to shelter.

Firm friends in this fragile moment,

like children on the playground.

You sit on the cushion, gentle tears

joining the judgeless rain.

Retreat – Return

Then: The peace, the stillness,

away from the strife.

Just the birdsong

making the body smile

at such loud, complex clarity

from such a small being.

The mind changes.

Now: Wishing the bloody birds

would just shut up,

stop their incessant, repetitive chirruping

of the same old tunes.

Taraloka's Mole

The mole is having a field day.

Hardy survivors, daisies, forget-me-nots

stand upright around the edges,

but not for long.

The mounds are filling the space

like a battleground.

I'll bet, now, you're expecting

another comic anecdote

about the gardener's war with mole.

His frantic search

for the perfect weapon

to end mole's encroachment.

Gas, smoke, traps.

You are perhaps imagining

his manic, mad-eyed efforts –

the gardener's, not the mole's –

to thwart his enemy.

How to protect

his hard-won creation,

the flat, perfect,

fretted-over,

tightly-controlled lawn.

Ah – you'd be wrong.

Here no-one finds

his tunnelling an affront,

a call to arms.

Here the gardener

likes to imagine mole's

oh so other

snuffling, small dark life,

his much-loved home,

with rising fellow-feeling

and gratitude for a world not flat.

Not flat at all.

Writing Class

'I'd like you to write about Doors.'

Through the keyhole I see

my little muse is digging in her heels,

blocking up her ears,

assuming a foetal position,

refusing my desperate pleas

to open the door.

Come out and play.

Neither carrot nor stick helps.

Cajoling notes through the letter box:

'It will be fun. Lots of praise.'

Bullying knocks, guilting whispers:

'It will humiliate you, writing nothing in class.'

Still no response,

perhaps just a little muffled sniggering.

I capitulate.

'We could write a poem called 'Muse'?

Will you come out then?'

Age

I drew my grandmother's face once.

It was a school project on 'Age'.

I glanced from her face to the paper many times,

made marks, aimed for detail,

then felt a sudden shame,

scrunched it into a ball

and binned it, said it was 'No good.'

I aged ten years right there when I saw

how carefully I'd captured all her lines,

but failed to draw her face.

Sweet Demon

You live with your tribe

in the deepest, tropical temple of my self.

You mean well.

You want me to survive.

You grow fat on the sweet leavings

of not enough, on a strict diet

of uncontrolled fear.

There's plenty to feed you,

but I mean to kill you,

with a fatal dose of love.

Haiku - ish

1.

The tiger crouches.

The pink cave shells of ears

tune to the moon's sound.

2.

On kitchen surface

liberally shedding hairs.

Oh! Poor sandwich!

3.

Mad tabby bullet

shoots through roaring traffic.

Pavement. Phew. Eight left.

4.

She toddled in as usual, but there was magic in the room.

She saw a wondrous thing. With eyes wide and arms outstretched

she shouted 'CAT!'

Connecting

I lost a sonnet many years ago.

I think I left it at another's house.

It was a heartfelt poem. I miss it, so

attempt remembrance of it, think of how

sometimes as I crouched, shaking, far from home,

I wrenched it out to help to keep me still.

My thoughts on something other, on this poem,

not on you, drunken, shrunken, miserably ill.

You, at our home, clenched like a hedgehog rolled,

so soft inside, but armoured to the hilt.

No-one could reach you, love, but untold

years I tried, failed, unwisely lived with guilt.

Now, owning the futility of this,

I've learned there is no simple, healing kiss.

Baby

I pace the gravel path in meditation,

stoop to cradle you,

feel your satin coolness,

gaze at subtle hues,

cream, milk white, budding pink.

Lower my face and breathe ...

you have no scent.

What a fool I am

to feel disappointment

in a rose.

Autumn Sleep

Sometimes I feel the clutch of fear

in arid times that I will never feel

the growing pains of poetry again.

Deceiving, wintry infertility.

What a fool I am to mistrust the seasons.

And now, this phrase, this bloody phrase

that has itched my mind for days,

chooses this hour,

this dark and peaceful hour,

to wake me with its starving cry

to be scratched into a poem.

Bleary-eyed, resentful,

I've staggered out of bed at your cry.

Unavoidable, tiny,

unavoidable, demanding poem.

Wasteland

To protect me

I cherish such fragments,

lines and verses,

wisdom from the bards,

creature comforts for the soul.

I fence them in my memory,

huddled to me,

murmuring community,

a shared fate,

shepherding me against life's wolfish mauling,

against my predatory fears,

stroking my joys,

licking my tears,

not against my ruin, but through it.

Ours

I'll never be Brian Wilson,

but his gut-sweet songs are mine.

I'll never be Rembrandt Van Rijn,

but his drawndeep faces are mine.

I'll never be Mary Oliver,

but her goosebump words are mine.

I'll never be Anthony Caro,

but his speaking spaces are our graces.

Boxes

Are you going to open the box?

Pandora's all–gifted, tempting,

leaving only expectations.

Can you believe there's something good in there?

Are you going to open the box?

Schröedinger's cat – alive or not,

needing finally to know – does he know?

Can you believe there's something good in there?

Siddhartha's simple tool box,

opened to the wide world.

No need to hesitate or fear.

Reach in joyfully. Find the nothing there.

Buddha Rupa

Sitting sturdy

in the lotus,

your perfect lap

can shelter me,

solacing,

holding me loosely

in the mudra

of your open hands.

Happening

Wound healing,

heart red to pink,

burning to cool,

puckered to smooth.

I'm watching

the miraculous,

redundantly,

doing nothing.

My thoughts, my thoughts

go round this carousel.

I think, I think

that they will never stop,

but this is just a fairground ride,

and there is stillness still inside.

A new little Upanishad

Buddha Day.

A question:

'What would you ask

the Buddha, if he walked in?'

Mind as blank

as the paper on my knees.

No question.

Just a clear view

of myself falling

in a little heap of gratitude

by his side.

Birthday Present

Gazing intently at this slightly blurred

black-and-white photo, a fiftieth-birthday present

from my oldest friend, I ask, 'Which one's me?'

I stare at ragamuffin infants, our St. David's Day.

Small boys dressed like old men.

Home-made Welsh hats, all different,

no glossy, standardized productions here.

'Guess who's me!' I say to present friends.

Only one can tell.

Memory brings to me the sight, the smell, the feel of ants

and cherry blossom on the low school wall.

The intense zoom of senses on the present moment

the very young can hold, a careless clarity.

That's me. Gone. A snapshot

The one who guessed right wasn't me.

Doing the Rounds

My Chart – Page 1. Thursday (Upswing)

1. Deafness – ongoing.

2. Osteoporosis – ongoing.

3. Tinnitus – fluctuating.

4. Epiretinal membrane – asymptomatic.

5. Verruca – pain on walking.

6. Old wound – itching.

7. Cold sore – fading.

Diagnosis: Dying.

My Chart – Page 2. Everyday (Downswing)

1. All of the above.

2. Many more and counting.

3. Fear.

Diagnosis: Living.

Rough with the smooth

I will write our love story in pencil, she said,

so it can be rubbed out with ease.

Let's not commit to pen.

The rubbing out

might make a hole in me.

Let us write it in water, he said.

Too soon the polished stone,

this mournful assonance

has haunted me, echoing in my spaces.

Too long the striving for perfection.

Life's ragged edges are magic,

are perfection.

Gravity

Bounded,

Sharply edged,

painfully defined,

I long to be

tumbling in Newton's ocean of truth,

smoothing me like his pebbles,

 or rather like his apple globe,

falling, blurring,

merging into the

boundless, groundless earth.

Post-atomic, subatomic,

part of the painless whole.

Screen

See this invisible chasm.

I am a child of peace.

Gunshots and screams are distant, unreal.

Carnage means images on tiny screens.

No tanks rumble into this quiet backwater.

Safe with untried pacifist notions, I watch you,

child of war,

muddied by loss, scorched by rage,

separated from me by the barbed-wire

no-man's land of experience.

You mouth your muffled message,

but I cannot hear.

Naming

I've always liked the idea of a

North American Indian name.

Something like *Dances With Wolves*;

something deeply meaningful,

attuned to nature.

Our names are so prosaic,

and, well, *Mary*'s never really felt like me.

What about *Swims With Dolphins*?

I could manage that.

Immerse myself in their watery home,

soothe my soul with their sleek empathy.

A touch clichéd, perhaps?

And I don't like to be wet.

I'd given up hope

until this cold winter's afternoon.

I held my breath

while you settled on my lap,

your paw on mine -

Mine, which still bears the scars of tooth and claw

from your fiercer days.

(A good Indian name should perhaps

entail some suffering, some bloodshed.)

We snooze in the half -light.

Your eyes are slightly open

but your nose is still. You are asleep.

You trust me now,

and we are warm and safe together.

I am *Dozes With Rabbit*.

Centre Stage

Some poems are shy, huddled in mind's corners,

hugging themselves, refusing to budge.

Some are teases, present themselves, promise much,

then withdraw, leaving raw fragments of broken syntax.

Some are bold, push themselves forward into the limelight,

oblivious of flaws, they strut their stuff. Like this one.

Mothering Sunday

Frail, bright paper hearts and flowers,

sent with love, indifference or pain,

camouflage the shriveled cord.

Lightweight helium balloons

float about the viscera and bones,

creaking when death's anguish looms,

Make us whimper for her

as you did, "Mum!",

as I will for you.

Germination

Everywhere the mind

has poemseeds.

Some never germinate –

too dry, too wet, not enough attention paid.

Some sprout regardless, an abundant harvest,

lush and nutritious.

Some jungle the mind out of,

and into, madness.

Some burst joyous surprise,

sunflowers, like magic.

Some grow strange, fungi,

disturbing the darkness.

Mine germinated in an Indian summer,

and grew just a few late blossoms,

in a sheltered corner;

some safe to eat, some less so.

Mary Griffiths

50

INDEX OF FIRST LINES

***